Sign Language
& School Activities

Bela Davis

Abdo Kids Junior
is an Imprint of Abdo Kids
abdobooks.com

abdobooks.com

Published by Abdo Kids, a division of ABDO, P.O. Box 398166, Minneapolis, Minnesota 55439.
Copyright © 2022 by Abdo Consulting Group, Inc. International copyrights reserved in all countries.
No part of this book may be reproduced in any form without written permission from the publisher.
Abdo Kids Junior™ is a trademark and logo of Abdo Kids.

Printed in the United States of America, North Mankato, Minnesota.

052021

092021

THIS BOOK CONTAINS
RECYCLED MATERIALS

Photo Credits: Shutterstock

Production Contributors: Teddy Borth, Jennie Forsberg, Grace Hansen

Design Contributors: Candice Keimig, Pakou Moua

Library of Congress Control Number: 2020947661

Publisher's Cataloging-in-Publication Data

Names: Davis, Bela, author.

Title: Sign language & school activities / by Bela Davis

Description: Minneapolis, Minnesota : Abdo Kids, 2022 | Series: Everyday sign language | Includes online
   resources and index.

Identifiers: ISBN 9781098207038 (lib. bdg.) | ISBN 9781098207878 (ebook) | ISBN 9781098208295
   (Read-to-Me ebook)

Subjects: LCSH: American Sign Language--Juvenile literature. | Schools--Juvenile literature. | Student life
   and customs--Juvenile literature. | Deaf--Means of communication--Juvenile literature. | Language
   acquisition--Juvenile literature.

Classification: DDC 419--dc23

Table of Contents

Signs and
School Activities 4

The ASL Alphabet! . .22

Glossary. 23

Index 24

Abdo Kids Code. 24

Signs and
School Activities

ASL is a visual language. There is a sign for every school activity!

SCHOOL

1. Hold one hand in front of body, palm facing up
2. Take the other hand, palm facing down, and clap the two hands together a couple of times

5

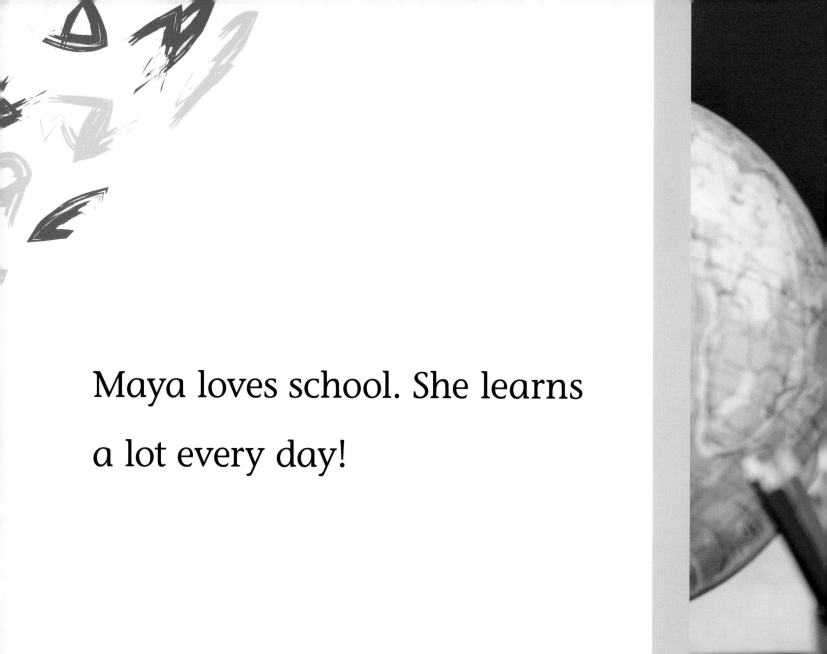

Maya loves school. She learns
a lot every day!

1. Bring one open hand to belly height, palm facing up

2. With other hand, pretend to grab something from open palm

3. Bring second hand up to forehead, like placing information into head

Mike is in the school choir.

He sings loudly.

SING

1. Bring a slightly curved, open hand close to the top of chest

2. Move hand outward and upward, like sound waves are going into the air

9

Dana likes story time. Her
teacher reads to the class.

READ

1. Hold one hand open at chest height
2. Make the "V" sign with the other hand
3. Point the two fingers of "V" hand at open palm and move up and down like scanning the page of a book

Luke's favorite class is art.

He loves to paint.

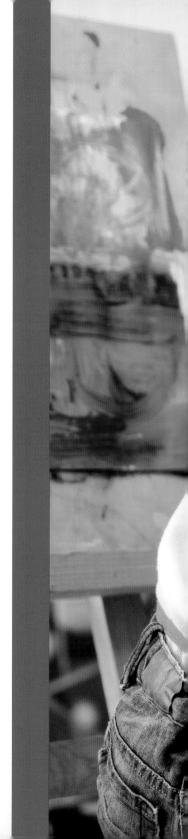

PAINT

1. Hold one hand straight up, thumb closest to body
2. With second hand, fingers together, brush fingertips up and down the palm of other hand

13

Ana liked science this week.

She got to build a robot!

BUILD

1. Hold hands in front of chest with palms facing down, fingers bent at knuckles
2. Place tips of right fingers over left hand
3. Place tips of left fingers over right hand
4. Repeat movements as hands build up toward head

Cara is good at math.

She loves to count!

COUNT

1. Bring one open hand to chest height, palm facing up, fingers away from body

2. Make the "F" sign with other hand

3. Take pointer finger and thumb of "F" hand and touch it to wrist of open hand and slide toward fingertips

Rob takes a test. He writes
his answers.

WRITE

1. Hold one hand open and at chest height, palm facing upward
2. With other hand, press pointer finger against thumb
3. Drag fingertips across open palm a few times

19

Everyone climbs the rope

in PE class.

CLIMB

1. Bring both hands up at chest height, palms facing out
2. Have each hand take turns moving up and grasping as if climbing a ladder

21

The ASL Alphabet!

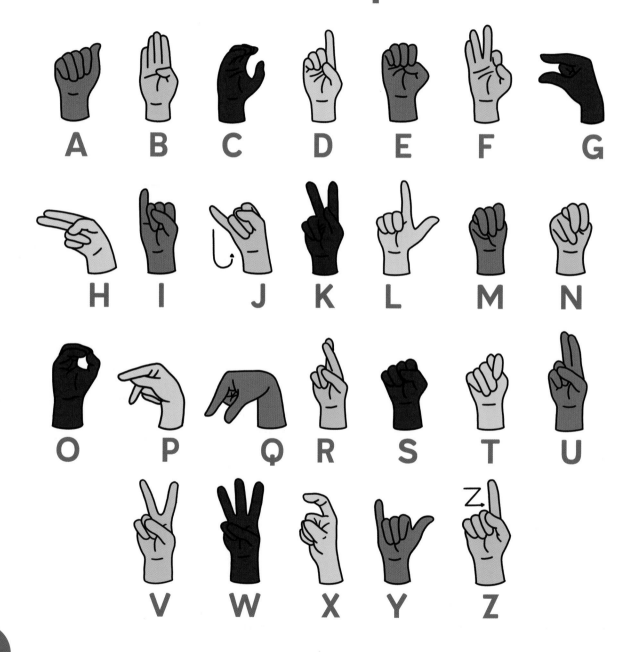

Glossary

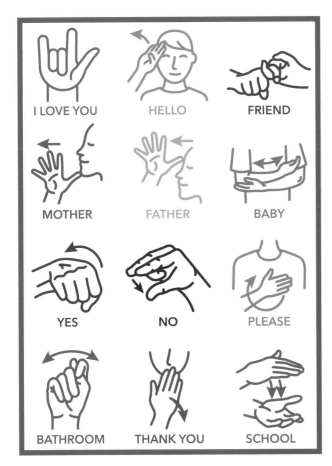

ASL
short for American Sign Language, a language used by many deaf people in North America.

PE
short for physical education, a class that teaches care and development of the body.

Index

American Sign Language (ASL) 4

art 12

building 14

choir 8

climbing 20

counting 16

learning 6

math 16

painting 12

Physical Education (PE) 20

reading 10

science 14

singing 8

writing 18

Abdo Kids ONLINE
FREE! ONLINE MULTIMEDIA RESOURCES

Visit **abdokids.com** to access crafts, games, videos, and more!

Use Abdo Kids code
ESK7038
or scan this QR code!